NINE SERIES

GenderFux

Jem Henderson
Jonathan Kinsman
JP Seabright

Published by Nine Pens

2022

www.ninepens.co.uk

All rights reserved: no part of this book may be reproduced without the publisher's permission.

The right of the authors to be identified as the authors of this work has been asserted by them in accordance with the Copyright, Designs and Patents Act 1988

ISBN: 978-1-7398274-1-0

NS 002

5   Birthday candles
6   Terms / Conditions
8   Fault\Lines
10 it's behind you
11 SHORT-CUTS
12 // delicate stitch //
13 Crocuta crocuta
14 otesánek (greedy guts)
16 *from* the Book of Demons
18 I dreamt I was a slag heap
20 the first pride was a riot
21 1994
22 Kayfabe
25 ninth circle
26 Etceterising
27 jack and jill went up the hill
29 entranced
30 myling
31 changeling in the cottage
33 exulansis
34 compositional
35 aubade with hyacinths
36 Age-Ache-Ask
38 Selkie
39 it's not you it's me
40 Variable Penetrance
41 some possible genders

Birthday candles

look closely now,
    can you see her, there in the flame?
        a swaying charcoal dancer,
            her arms raised high
          in the ecstatic conflagration,
this pink and white spiral staircase
collapsing beneath her,
    and across the glazed skyline
        every tower goes up in reverence,
            the darkness alight with song
                babylon burning
            for your sake.
        don't think of your father
          ascending floor after floor
      wax ceilings collapsing
    over his shoulders
     sweet powder in his eyes as he
        searches, sugar in his lungs.
           he's here, match pinched
        between finger and thumb,
     laughing through
        a flat happy birthday.
          dear amy,
              make a wish.

	Sky	Shadow	Earth	Body
Articulate	she smiles on those who are loved & unloved / the sun / but it feels like a mother's hug / only when you have one	the shadow says / I'm really not myself today / or any day	I feel planetary motion / my scream / pulls up trees / by their roots	today I made sure I ate well / exercised / moved through 28 points of articulation / called my friends / forgave my ex boyfriend / knowing his motives / shrouded in myth & conjecture
Lift	I raise my hands to the firmament / palms up / holding everything / the whole weight of the air	use tarot cards / i-ching / the spittle string from mouths of lovers / lift the veil / peek / underneath / at all the treasures / I have been hiding	mountain shifts / upwards through the crust / erupt in tiger lava / down towards me / the only thing to hold onto / is my cock	*asking for help is a weakness / so put your back into it / your legs / your eyes / your tongue / raise your voice in lamentation / while hormones crumble your bones*

Gender	the moon is a man / fat & full of mortal lusting / the sun / she gifts us with burnt skin / pink kisses & scorn	the chattering keeps my curtains closed / hiding from the black & white	before I was an alder / I was dancing queen / I was a willow / I was catkin & seed / spilled over the fertile ground	today I held a pen & wrote a poison / yes father, I understand / yesterday I clawed fingers down my legs / convinced the wound hates me
Revolution ((-))	the man/moon / angry faced & smiling / says we like neat endings, but often have to live / with watching them come around again	armed / with revolvers / shotguns / the relics of this war / they come as a horde / to drive us out of town / out of love / I slip away / into the dark	blood on the soil / feeds blossom on the trees / mono no aware / just smell that springtime	yesterday I held my breasts in my hand & cried / morphed / into something / forever beautiful

Fault\Lines

"Well, you've always been you dear" was all my mother could say when I told her I was gay. My father said nothing, he didn't come to the phone. I expect he was wondering: 'First my brother now my daughter, what have I done to deserve such pain? Where did we go so wrong? Whose fault was it? Who should we blame? Is there a degenerate gene running in the family? Is it because we let her wear jeans and play football? Is it because she cut her hair short that one time and I beat her with my belt so she wouldn't dare again? Should we have insisted on more dolls, more dresses, more activities that weren't playing football or the guitar, neither suitable for a girl. Should we have let her to go to Brownies or Guides or those other things that schoolgirls like to do?'

After a short pause in which there was nothing that one I said nothing, since could say to my mother's dismissive response, she added: "*Do you think your brother might be...* also?" She couldn't say the word, couldn't allow it to sit in her mouth, trip over her tongue, taint her diction, her sense of self. How will this impact on her husband, local school teacher, what will people think? They'd only just been accepted into the inner sanctum of the local Methodist Church. Another dirty family secret. It's on a need to know basis, and no one needs to know.

My mother's only other words on the matter, a few months later when I saw my parents for the first time as a self-confessed lesbian, were: "*I'm just disappointed that I'll never be a grandmother.*" Nothing about my girlfriend, my potential future parenthood, nothing like: 'as long as you're happy that's all that matters', nothing about me and my life. Has that changed in the intervening twenty five years? It has not. Who's fault is that? I wonder.

it's behind you

PRINCIPAL BOY:

(you can be him as long as they're laughing; as long as you dance in your stockings, belt tight to your gift-wrapped waist; as long as your mother paints her face for the back row, cock curtained; as long as she sings her bawdy bassline, pressgangs men to her bosom; as long as you kiss a real girl, slim as a wish, tongue and all, saliva stage-lit; as long as they're laughing)

SHORT-CUTS

Request a compromise cut: accepted,
appropriate for work, meetings, clients,
yet in keeping with my identity/
/personality/sexual preference.

(Delete whichever is applicable.)
Fetch the mirror of misunderstanding,
always disappointed by the outcome,
how they feminise my short, back and sides.

My reticence and capitulation,
society's straightlaced expectations,
how my identity is still defined
by the shape and shortness of my haircut.

Just a little bit more off the back please,
if you don't mind, yes a bit shorter still.

// delicate stitch //

the white of my lace cotton socks // black rubber plimsolls // squeak on the varnished floor // yellow felt tip lines on cream recycled paper // fragile followed with freshly sharpened pencil // learn my ABCs

my first kiss behind the huts at school // his cheeks sucked in tight to make a tiny lipless pout // smashing my face on the paving // leaving fat drops blooming like red flowers on grey stone // three stitches

a second kiss in the garden // her pale body delicate like antique lace under my hand // fleeing my mother's house // her sightless eyes // her needle fingers

my rattling cough // mould trapped in tender lace of lung // a parade of men with flaccid dicks and fleshy bellies // no money // no food // the lace is my arm // delicately sliced

the lace is my wedding dress // the lace is the cowl around my baby face // audibly popping at quarter to midnight // the lace is my crumbling marriage // keeping me in place

Crocuta crocuta

                                            androgen exposure
                                female hyenas
           muscular   aggressive
                                         higher rank than
males   dominant   alpha
females   higher levels of
androgen
                                lick   clitorises of
higher-ranked   females   submission
obedience   females   lick each other's clitorises

all males lick   clitorises of dominant females
females   not lick   penises   males
are
    lowest rank

otesánek (greedy guts)

anything can be a child, if you squint,

>so they swaddle the swollen stump,
>bind its leaves up in bunches,
>set it out in the garden
>in a little pink sunhat

even as it weeps

>its gnarled fat fists beating against
>mother's breast, its fissure mouth
>clamped tight, refuses to suckle
>until the surgeon cuts a wider
>wooden grimace to force the teat inside.

milk, it's only word,

>screams *milk, milk milk*
>and snatches up the neighbour's cat,
>sicks bloody froth against the muslin
>that first tooth a nasty splinter
>sunk tight in *pussy pussy pussy.*
>its chest warps, distends and yowls,
>so father sits it upside-down

says *you have had*

>*your pretty pussy, settle, fucking settle*
>but now the stump has the colic

sets upon the paperboy,
a perfect little beast that fills the throat
as he goes down and a cry goes up of
paper boy milk boy pussy boy
while all its writhing branches crack
to burst its frilly dresses,
ribbons, lace and thread
meant to bind this whitsun demon
tattered on the lawn
and it sprints naked for the gate, needs

a taste of flesh

to satiate the hunger before it thinks
of sleep but daddy's got the axe out,
shrieks *we'll have ourselves a bonfire*
and gives chase about the garden
while mummy sits and sobs
for the child she wanted
and not the child she got.

now

he's barbequing dinner
and she's digging out a stone
a lump of orange brick buried
in the flowerbed and she
swaddles this instead
says *this one's a son, love.*

at least we're not alone.

From the Book of Demons
Chapter 1

1. I am summoned to see you. 2. I enter the room we use for our meetings. Sitting on a chair on the raised platform at the far end, you are lost in prayer. 3. Eyes open, palms raised, seeking guidance from heaven. 4. I try not to stare. 5. I sway slightly, my balance askew. I am drunk. I have been swimming in alcohol all afternoon. 6. I have done my best to disguise this. To hide the fact. To mask the smell. 7. I am good at hiding things from people.

Chapter 2

1. "Why do you do it?" you ask. I shrug. I do not know why. 2. "I can see evil spirits at work in you." 3. I turn to look for them. I have suspected this for some time. 4. "I can see them now, demons dancing around you." 5. I do not know how to answer this. I say nothing. 6. "Come closer." 7. I do so slowly, warily, but seeking release. I concentrate on the cross behind your head to keep my path true. My legs buckle, the pressure in the room is unbearable. It is easy to kneel down before you. 8. You reach your hand out to me.

Chapter 3

1. "Oh Lord, cast out the evil spirits that plague this child. Cast them out Lord and flood her heart with your love. Show her how to resist temptation and help her to keep to the righteous path though obeying your will. In the name of our Lord Jesus Christ." 2. Your hands are small, but your grip is firm. 3. You are standing now, my head in your hands, clasped tight, as if it might escape. 4. I am trembling. Tears are streaming down my face. I am not sure if this is the Holy Spirit or the 42% proof. 5. You are speaking in tongues. A language I cannot understand, but its meaning is clear from your grip on my head.

Chapter 4

1. Your husband enters the room. The charismatic leader of the evangelical cult I have been hijacked into during the hollow vulnerability of this post-traumatic abyss. 2. It is an ambush. Prearranged. 3. This is not an opportunity for counsel and prayer, but a forcing out of all my evil. 4. An exorcism. 5. He stands over me pushing down hard on my shoulders, as if I might struggle. 6. I do not struggle. I know it will be useless. Like the time before. And the time before that. 7. Perhaps they imagine a wild beast inside me refusing to let go. They restrain my body accordingly. 8. But there is no wild beast, no evil spirit. 9. There is only a young girl, barely an adult. Abused and confused, seeking solace in alcohol and sex.

Chapter 5

1. Please make it stop. 2. They shout their biblical obscenities at me and my demons. With all good intent I'm sure. 3. He stands over me, forcing me down, triggering the trauma of a rape too recent to have had any hope of recovering from. 4. Too raw to have processed, except with liquid oblivion. 5. Verily I say unto you, it had started to heal. Through a love that finally spoke her name. 6. A love that would deny me the sanctifying blood of the Lamb. 7. A love that is evil and shameful. And the work of demons.

Chapter 6

1. I weep. 2. You stop. Eventually. 3. I do not know how long it lasted. Minutes. Hours. A lifetime. 4. I am spent, exhausted. Prostrate on the floor. The room still spinning around me. 5. For despite my drunken struggle with the demons forced upon me, by your lord and saviour, not mine, I feel guilty and ashamed. 6. You have made me dirty and defiled again. 7. You have exorcised my body and my soul.

I dreamt I was a slag heap

once I was a man
Star Trek obsessed
hand on
hard dick
eyes on supple body
refining the salt muck of me
savoured by the drain

once I was a cam girl
running my hands
over my *Big Beautiful Tits*
the white ring light
sparkling like a geode
turning circles for the camera
on my unmade bed

eyes, eyes, eyes, eyes
like galgalim
golden wheels whirl and spin
watching my every move

open up the chat box
send a red heart emoji
to each and every
starstruck cockroach

once I was ore
quarried out

slag

once I was a cricket
stridulation wings
like chafing thighs

maybe I am a man dreaming he is a cricket
or a woman dreaming she is a man
or androgene, dreaming of the binary

or
  or
    and/or
       or

the first pride was a riot

from the horizon it must look like the end of all things —

conflagration, orange on black;

            a contortion of limbs,
              one moment pulling in unison
    and the next whirling against each other;

       furious flesh
         and its sweet bellow;

                a piano's viking funeral,
            attended only by torsos,
              the mourners' legs swallowed
                    up in noise —
all are welcome:
                you curios;
                  you nameless of no-place;
      you made inside out,
            holding your entrails in your hands —
            turn them in at the cloakroom;

we'll watch your things while you dance.
marsha is giving out shots

                that taste like blood in your teeth;
                  there's one for you.

    drink deep.
        sing like a sword in the forge.

1994

The line in that song where she sings   *You're a girl & I'm a boy*
did more for my gender identity   than anything before or since
This was 1994   just 21 & finding out
who I was & am   who I love & how
at the Uni queer disco before   the T was added to the LGB Soc
my third girlfriend was President of   standing watching waiting
checking everyone out just in case   searching not for perfection
nor protection but a palpable   sense of validation
This was 1994   halfway through the shame of Section 28
I went to my first Gay Pride that year   in Brockwell Park
here I found my self my family   my people my Protection
if & when I needed it   *You're a girl & I'm a boy*
This was 1994   when Currie's law failed to pass
the gay age of consent stalled at 18   but no age of consent
for lesbians   still we did not exist
This was 1994   when Jarman died of AIDS
before antiretrovirals came in   & we watched *Blue*
in pieces at the Phoenix Cinema   *You're a girl & I'm a boy*
is my manifesto for love   though sometimes we are both boys
& sometimes   we are both girls too
but I am not fixed   I am a state of flux
I am GenderFux   I am not one thing
or another   alternating like electricity
I am not sometimes this & sometimes that   not either/or
I am fluid & peculiar   I am everything at once
bubbles rising   to the surface of a lake
confetti dancing   in the slipstream

Kayfabe

Hulk Hogan body slams Andre the Giant in 80s Detroit in front of 93,173 screaming fans, ending Andre's 15 year undefeated streak.

//

In 1985, my mother holds onto my pink screaming girl body after 36 hours of labour and a c-section *ruins* hers.

//

kayfabe n. (in professional wrestling) the fact or convention of presenting staged performances as genuine or authentic.

//

At ten years old, I first cut off all my hair. The kids at school leered *are you a boy or a girrrrll?* Are you a boy or a girl? YES.

//

When I cut off my hair for the first time it makes me feel like a warrior in a battle I don't know I'll be fighting for the rest of my life.

//

1998's Hell In A Cell match ends between Mankind and The Undertaker. Mick Foley won't stay down even after being thrown off the top of the cage.

//

Somedays, my gender feels like a prison. I can slip through the bars like in X-Men. Turn to water. Gender fluid.

//

The Wrestlemania women's event between Sasha Banks and Bianca Belair in 2021 is only the second female-led main event ever.

//

2021 has already seen at least 28 transgender or gender nonconforming people fatally shot or killed by other violent means in the US.

//

what the fuck is wrong with me I scream at my friend, smashing the mirror on her living room wall.

//

Stone Cold Steve Austin smashes The Rock with a chair in 2001. The referee counts 1, 2, 3.

Austin 3:16

//

My hair is short, bleached white blond in 2001, so I can look like the lead singer of The Offspring. It's the year I got kicked out of home.

//

I'm 16 and I'm trying on another new identity. Heel turn. Heel turned. I'm not as bad as my mother says I am.

//

At Wrestlemania 25 a top rope moonsault puts The Heartbreak Kid in the arms of the Undertaker who plants him with a Tombstone piledriver.

//

Homelessness puts me in the arms of men, good and bad. One holds me through the night while I cry for my lost childhood, another drinks until he doesn't care if I want sex or not. I owe him.

//

I'm chanting ringside, yelling for the man dressed in only a white shirt and underpants.

//

36 years wrestling. Face or heel. Girl or boy.

ninth circle

an estimated
          thirty-seven
                    trillion cells
     collectively hallucinate my existence
          by means of a faint electrical current
                    conducted through
                              a slab of wet bacon;
just a single line item
in a system of infinite permutations.

          an ovum falls from the body
               no, it cries,
               smothering itself
                    in the cotton pad.
                         a whole clot of haematids
          protesting
               but the biological imperative
          tumble as lemmings.

the insular cortex lights up,
     synapses glowing,
     fleshy live wires
                    raining sparks
                         into the cockpit.
                    there is no protocol for this:
          the first failure
                    in a three-point-five-billion-year
                              chain of success.

     my womb whispers
          life gives you a single task —

     but i don't listen.
          i am selfish like that.

Etceterising

      here I stand before you with
all my etcetera etcetera
      this effeminate ephemera
tanked up to my tits on testosterone
      my clit is hard gnawed raw as a bone
& did you happen to know
      that the clitoris is the same length
as the average flaccid penis
      four inches from hood to glans
to the end of my lucky wishbone
      & my corpus cavernosum
is just that – cavernous - all tucked up
      next to those unwanted eggs
all fucked up between your legs
      so whenever I've worn a fake dick
it's an extension of my real one
      & however I choose to decorate
my mons pubis with whatever & etcetera
      know that you have made me
into a thing of wanting
      & I feel every single one of
those 8000 sensory nerve endings

jack and jill went up the hill

jack or jill went up the hill. jack. jill. uphill.
jack swaggers, scratches his beard.
does 100 squats and 97 press ups,
pushing back from the slope of green grass.
jill looks on, unimpressed.

jill goes up the hill. up. hill. her heels
can't take it. she takes them off. leaves them,
beige and lonely, metres apart. unable
to hop the distance between them.

jack and jill went up the hill.
jack jill went up the hill.
jack. jill. jackjill.
up hill. overhead. swapped outfits
and came down as each other.
jack as jill. jill as jack. jilljack.

jack and jill went up the hill, stretching
their legs after a drug-fuelled night out.
sex. cocaine. a memory of a naked
stranger's back.
the inevitable comedown.

jack goes up the hill
comes down as jill
a face of spirit gum, dermablend
and glitter / glitter / glitter.

jack went up the hill, tripped up, fell down.

jill went up the hill and came down after
listening to jack talk about jordan peterson
and his lobsters for 45 minutes straight,
unable to get
a
word
in
edgeways.

jack and jill went up the hill. jill gave jack
a handjob on a tartan blanket. jack got off.
jack off. jill.
jill did not.

entranced

One is not born, but rather becomes, a woman
        and you look so becoming tonight

We unmake ourselves and each other
        under filthy fluorescent light

Our various bodies are uncharted territory
        you take cover as I take flight

There was no agenda when I met you, no tickbox
        our manifesto is one of sexual sleight

And for all our exits and entrances
        I am still entranced by you
                sometimes   ☒
                completely   ☒
                in an instant   ☒

myling

take the next breath —
    it is a gift, for you — this staccato
puncture of the air
    grants another moment longer.

but you look at your boy born blue
    and know he will not last.
if it comes to pass that you must bury me,
    set a coffin bell upright,

let it ring out brilliant
    across a clear summer evening,
my own name rising,
    a ghost in your throat.

do i already haunt you, some
    bloody spectre of beds
and bathrooms? or does it ache
    too much to look?

changeling in the cottage

stolen milk breath from the cot
replaced that mewling pudgy girl
with this - it does not cry in the night
              like she did
only stares at you, it's eyes
              blue as clear dusk

you gathered up
the mushrooms stewed
in tea until the good came out
through shimmering waves

      and a clarity
             like a hand to the throat
      they showed you

father rocks it gently
        although it does not sleep
you hold it to your chest
and try to feed even though
its grasping fists
and toothed mouth fill you
      with grey
            filthy waves

it grows - you feed it nuts and berries
meat and milk of the goat
honeycomb so sweet
it makes your jaw hurt
      sweets for the sweet

anything to stop the bitter words it speaks

it doesn't play with other girls
preferring to fight with sticks-as-swords
tumble down until its knees are bloody
        and you have to clean them with boiled water
            say *this might hurt*
not expecting the crimson of the blood

it comes to you and father
        says it *does not belong*
        says it's *not a girl*
you knew all along
praying for the day
that it'd go to its kind
        and bring your baby girl back

exulansis[1]

        a tripping hazard   the chairs pulled out we sit at the table   while my tongue writes the alphabet of this   our civilization

        we're holding hands   across the coffee cups arms outstretched   across a keening desert   wind

whipping the sand   into the ghosts   of djinn   and cake

        i make a list   mountains   with dark untrodden summits   rivers so wide   they   look   like seas   peninsulas   with   fingers outstretched
          i talk myself a map

        i'm drawing   in   the   foam of   the   waves   and   coffee   my voice echos   across   valleys   a scream underwater   a nightmare
              here   be

---

[1] *n. the tendency to give up trying to talk about an experience because people are unable to relate to it*

compositional

at first the only place i wear it is to bed,
wade out into it like a roman bath, the spring of it
rumbling up from my bones, crystalline and fresh.
the cathedral of the human mouth has the best acoustics,
lingers on those wide open vowels, that *o*
you suck into those rounded depths the first note
in the chord of my name. i offer you this
so you can return it, call and response.
jonathan, a coin fed to the coffer during hymn,
sweet charity, blessed gift bestowed by the lord himself.
your tongue licks at the thorn in my middle, soothes
this unfathomable wound. i have not discarded love,
just cheap romance, these girlish trappings. i never
spoke the language, prefer a harsh germanic *n*
clipped and certain of its ends and its beginnings.

aubade with hyacinths

stop me, darling.
forbid the morning
and shackle me to the sunset.

>each dawn i am
a handful of blue petals
undone in the wind

but hold me.
keep me in this body
a little longer.

>the boy broken open
begging *anything,*
but alas,

his ending is
already in motion
blunt and heavy.

>my light,
there is a goodbye
in the pink sunrise.

Age-Ache-Ask

    I age
I can feel it
    tree roots slowly crumbling
    frost cracking up a windowpane
My skin becomes loose
perhaps I have reduced in size
    in stature
    in strength
My face becomes lined
    with tributaries
    of perpetual tiredness

    I ache
But worse is that I have somehow
    become *more* woman
    I wasn't expecting this
I bleed more often not less
when before it was easy to forget
    My monthly cycle never in sync
    with the moon or my lovers
It used to skip and sail on regardless
    I thought myself lucky
    to be free of such femaleness

    I ask
Why now as a newborn parent
    I finally feel my ovulation
    a small toad squatting in my side
There are only three times I ever
feared to miss my period

concerned to have been
contaminated or impregnated
Only one of those was consensual
    but now my monthly bleeds me dry
    reminding me of all my frailties

Selkie

how old were you when you knew you were other?

as old as the sea shore / made & remade by the tide twice a day / sand and loam / chalk crumbled to reveal / brachiopods and bivalves / echinoid and ammonite

state your name for the tape

siren / selkie / mermaid / fish wife / seal / kin to Orkney / mistress / the sea / rumour / false treasure at the end of a rainbow / vicious rocks in the blinding fog / traveller from the upper cretaceous / microplastic devourer / lighthouse keeper / puddle watcher

what will you become?

corporeal / metamorph / transmute / dull lead to shining gold / slippery fins to trembling legs and cunt / he takes his little finger and hooks me / like a prize carp / 'til I slap and squirm like a fish out of water / in my wanting / slip between the covers of his bed / make him the one to gasp for breath / lick the salt / off my skin / becoming / only in this moment / woman it's not you it's me

kiss me, hold me, tie me in knots.
take my breasts for risk of cancer,
replace them with silicone chicken fillets.
take my dick, go on, take it.
lay down next to me, touch me
my smooth skin, my stubble
rasps under your fingertips.

get high with me, laugh until our breath stops
keep me under stairs, locked in the closet
keep me black and white & pinafored
I'm here to serve. hold me up in ray of sunlight,
glittering gold and throwing shapes
across the dancefloor. I'm ballroom.
I'm speedqueen. I'm a line of coke,
a wobble of ketamine,
queer and unending.
bruises under makeup
red lipstick pouting,
an orange clownfish, shifting
gender iridescence.

bring me flowers. bring me chocolate.
stand over my grave and ugly cry.
piss pretty on my headstone. tell everyone
that you loved me. tell everyone
that you hated the way I wrinkled my nose
& that I was always fucking right,
& that you didn't even know who I was.

Variable Penetrance

I am a construct / of parts
  / dissembling / reassembling
not one thing / I am everything
  / all potentialities / nothing
neutral / neutered / nubile
  / a pot of possibilities / at the end
of the rainbow / some days
  / I wear all genders at once / other days
none / but I do not / feel naked
  / my blood / my identity / my bones & limbs
my breasts / my cock / my cunt / my clit
  / my father's hateful / nose & eyebrows
my mother's fateful / cleft chin & neuroses
  / I do not define myself / nor my inheritance
my variable penetrance

some possible genders

ballboy / girl guide / motherfucker / ratking / her majesty / emcee / ladykiller / ex-lover / godfather / grave cleric / cock - jokey / cruel mistress / bootlicker / jobsworth / test-tube baby yummy-mummy / yuppie scum / anti-vaxxer / here-for-a-good-time-not-a-long-time / do-you-have-a-light? / skintight / payload / homonym / i-have-work-tomorrow / cheat code / phone-it-in / neo-liberal / ex-catholic / frankie-says-relax / lie-back-and-think-of-england / bonus track / urban myth / past-due / prosecco-flavoured / panic attack / panopticon / curbstomp / deck chair / semaphore / high-vis / give-'em-an-inch / kettling / do-you-hear-the-people-sing? / if-the-glove- fits / o negative / may-have-had-sex-with-a-man-who-may-have-had-sex-with-a-man / hypodermic / intravenous / transubstantiation / scientific method / wisdom teeth / bathroom stall / eurovision / cosmic latte / can-i-take-your-order-please? / vip / wall-to-wall / on the boil / hands up / i-don't-wanna -fight-tonight / baby-it's-cold-outside / two kids in a trenchcoat / pyromaniac / piggyback / you-spin-me-right-round / i-do-believe -in-fairies / don't-call-me-brave / feeling lucky / fire drill / union rep / back-in-my-day / what-can-i-say? / lick-it-up / i'm-not-bad -i'm-just-drawn-this-way / ekphrastic / biblically accurate / programming error / education-education-education / section 28 / cursive / 5 GCSEs A*-C / day release / thought police / did-you-take-your-medication? / temporal paradox / meatsuit / messiah / mop and bucket / salt on the rim / strangler fig / depth charges / my-profit-on-it / supermarket own-brand / sugar-coated / suburban monstrosity / fixer-upper / it-gets -better / point-on-the-diagram / outlier-who-should-not-have-been-counted / unexplained phenomena / gaping maw / astronaut / brilliant / brief / being

Acknowledgements

'birthday candles' is by Jonathan Kinsman.

'Terms and Conditions' is by Jem Henderson and was first published in the Babel Tower Notice Board, 2021.

'Fault\Lines' is by JP Seabright.

'it's behind you' is by Jonathan Kinsman.

'SHORT-CUTS' is by JP Seabright.

'//delicate stitch//' is by Jem Henderson.

'Crocuta crocuta' is by JP Seabright and is an erasure of text found in the Wikipedia entry on the clitoris of the spotted hyena.

'otesánek (greedy guts)' is by Jonathan Kinsman and uses the Czech fairy tale of the same name as its basis.

'*from* the Book of Demons' is by JP Seabright.

'I dreamt I was a slag heap' is by Jem Henderson and references Star Trek, the greatest TV show of all time.

'the first pride was a riot' is by Jonathan Kinsman and references Marsha P. Johnson, a queer liberation activist widely believed to have thrown a shot-glass at the start of the Stonewall riots.

'1994' is by JP Seabright. The line "You're a girl and I'm a boy" is from the song *Protection* by Everything But The Girl. The poem references Section 28 of the Local Government Act 1988 which prohibited local authorities from "intentionally prompt[ing] homosexuality", as well as the proposed Amendment to the Sexual Offences Act 1967, brought by the MP Edwina Currie in 1994 in an attempt to equal the age of consent. Derek Jarman the film director, his film *Blue*, and the Phoenix Cinema in Leicester are also referenced.

'kayfabe' is by Jem Henderson and references a series of WWE matches from 1987, 1998, 2001 and 2021.

'ninth circle' is by Jonathan Kinsman and takes its title from Dante Aleghieri's *Inferno*.

'etceterising' is by JP Seabright. The corpus cavernosum is the erectile tissue that forms both the penis and the clitoris.

'jack and jill went up the hill' is by Jem Henderson.

'entranced' is by JP Seabright and quotes from Simone de Beauvoir's book, The Second Sex

'myling' is by Jonathan Kinsman and takes its title from the child ghosts of Scandinavian folklore.

'changeling in the cottage' is by Jem Henderson.

'exulanis' is by Jem Henderson and takes its title from an entry in the Dictionary of Obscure Sorrows.

'compositional' is by Jonathan Kinsman.

'aubade with hyacinths' is by Jonathan Kinsman and makes reference to the Greek myth of the death of Hyacinthus.

'Age-Ache-Ask' is by JP Seabright.

'Selkie' is by Jem Henderson.

'it's not you, it's me' is by Jem Henderson.

'Variable Penetrance' is by JP Seabright and takes its title from genetics where the number of individuals carrying a particular variant of a gene expresses an identifiable trait, in this case, the cleft chin.

'some possible genders' is by Jonathan Kinsman and takes lines from: Les Misérables, the lifestyle section of the NHS pre-blood donation questionnaire, Merry Christmas (I don't wanna fight tonight) by The Ramones, Baby It's Cold Outside by Frank Loesser, You Spin Me Round (Like A Record) by Dead or Alive, Peter Pan, Heathers, Who Framed Roger Rabbit?, a 1996 speech by Tony Blair, The Tempest and the "Spiders Georg" meme.

The Poets:

Jonathan Kinsman (he/him) is a polyamorous, bisexual, transmasculine poet from Greater Manchester. His poems have been published widely, including in *Butcher's Dog, fourteen poems, Poetry Wales* and *Under the Radar*. His debut pamphlet *&* was joint-winner of the Indigo Dreams Pamphlet Prize 2017 and his second, *witness,* was published by Burning Eye in 2020.

Jem Henderson (she/they) is a genderqueer poet from Leeds, UK with an MA in Creative Writing from York St. John University. They have been published in Civic Leicester's Streetcake, Dreich, Full House Literary, and recently won a Creative Future award for underrepresented writers. A book, An Othered Mother is due out in 2022 from Nine Pens.

JP Seabright (she/they) is a queer writer living in London. Their debut poetry pamphlet, *Fragments from Before the Fall: An Anthology in Post-Anthropocene Poetry* is **published by Beir Bua Press**. Their debut prose chapbook NO HOLDS BARRED is out early 2022 from **Lupercalia Press**. They were nominated for a Pushcart Prize in October 2021.

www.ingramcontent.com/pod-product-compliance
Lightning Source LLC
Chambersburg PA
CBHW020037120526
44589CB00032B/612